Euthyphro

Plato

© 2022 Culturea Editions
Illustration de couverture : © domaine public
Edition : Culturea, le patrimoine des lettres (Hérault, 34)
Contact : infos@culturea.fr
Retrouvez notre catalogue sur http://culturea.fr
Imprimé en Allemagne par Books on Demand
In de Tarpen 42, Norderstedt
Design typographique : Derek Murphy
Layout : Reedsy (https://reedsy.com/)
ISBN : 9791041941285
Dépôt légal : Décembre 2022

literature, in English, to free and easy access of those wishing to make use of them.

Euthyphro   by Plato

This Euthyphro and Socrates are represented as meeting in the porch of the King Archon. (Compare Theaet.) Both have legal business in hand.

Socrates is defendant in a suit for impiety which Translated by Benjamin Jowett Meletus has brought against him (it is remarked by the way that he is not a likely man himself to INTRODUCTION.

have brought a suit against another); and Euthyphro too is plaintiff in an action for murder, which he has IN THE MENO, Anytus had parted from Socrates with brought against his own father. The latter has origi-the significant words: 'That in any city, and par-nated in the following manner:—A poor dependant ticularly in the city of Athens, it is easier to do men of the family had slain one of their domestic slaves harm than to do them good;' and Socrates was in Naxos. The guilty person was bound and thrown anticipating another

opportunity of talking with into a ditch by the command of
Euthyphro's fa-him. In the Euthyphro, Socrates is awaiting his trial
ther, who sent to the interpreters of religion at Ath-for impiety. But
before the trial begins, Plato would ens to ask what should be done
with him. Before like to put the world on their trial, and convince the
messenger came back the criminal had died them of ignorance in that
very matter touching from hunger and exposure.

which Socrates is accused. An incident which may This is the origin
of the charge of murder which perhaps really have occurred in the
family of Euthyphro brings against his father. Socrates is con-
Euthyphro, a learned Athenian diviner and sooth-fident that before
he could have undertaken the sayer, furnishes the occasion of the
discussion.

responsibility of such a prosecution, he must have 3

Euthyphro

been perfectly informed of the nature of piety ther with murder,' may
be a single instance of and impiety; and as he is going to be tried for
piety, but can hardly be regarded as a general impiety himself, he
thinks that he cannot do definition.

better than learn of Euthyphro (who will be ad-Euthyphro replies,
that 'Piety is what is dear mitted by everybody, including the judges,
to be to the gods, and impiety is what is not dear to an
unimpeachable authority) what piety is, and them.' But may there not
be differences of opin-what is impiety. What then is piety?

ion, as among men, so also among the gods? Es-Euthyphro, who, in the abundance of his knowl-pecially, about good and evil, which have no fixed edge, is very willing to undertake all the respon-rule; and these are precisely the sort of differ-sibility, replies: That piety is doing as I do, pros-ences which give rise to quarrels. And therefore ecuting your father (if he is guilty) on a charge what may be dear to one god may not be dear to of murder; doing as the gods do—as Zeus did to another, and the same action may be both pious Cronos, and Cronos to Uranus.

and impious; e.g. your chastisement of your fa-Socrates has a dislike to these tales of mythol-ther, Euthyphro, may be dear or pleasing to Zeus ogy, and he fancies that this dislike of his may (who inflicted a similar chastisement on his own be the reason why he is charged with impiety.

father), but not equally pleasing to Cronos or

'Are they really true?' 'Yes, they are;' and Uranus (who suffered at the hands of their sons).

Euthyphro will gladly tell Socrates some more Euthyphro answers that there is no difference of them. But Socrates would like first of all to of opinion, either among gods or men, as to the have a more satisfactory answer to the question, propriety of punishing a murderer. Yes, rejoins

'What is piety?' 'Doing as I do, charging a fa-Socrates, when they know him to be a murderer; 4

Euthyphro

but you are assuming the point at issue. If all because it is dear to them. Here then appears to the circumstances of the case are considered, are be a contradiction,—Euthyphro has been giving you able to show that your father was guilty of an attribute or accident of piety only, and not murder, or that all the gods are agreed in ap-the essence. Euthyphro acknowledges himself proving of our prosecution of him? And must you that his explanations seem to walk away or go not allow that what is hated by one god may be round in a circle, like the moving figures of liked by another? Waiving this last, however, Daedalus, the ancestor of Socrates, who has com-Socrates proposes to amend the definition, and municated his art to his descendants.

say that 'what all the gods love is pious, and Socrates, who is desirous of stimulating the in-what they all hate is impious.' To this Euthyphro dolent intelligence of Euthyphro, raises the ques-agrees.

tion in another manner: 'Is all the pious just?'

Socrates proceeds to analyze the new form of

' Yes.' 'Is all the just pious?' 'No.' 'Then what the definition. He shows that in other cases the part of justice is piety?' Euthyphro replies that act precedes the state; e.g. the act of being car-piety is that part of justice which 'attends' to ried, loved, etc. precedes the state of being car-the gods, as there is another part of justice which ried, loved, etc., and therefore that which is dear

'attends' to men. But what is the meaning of to the gods is dear to the gods because it is first

'attending' to the gods? The word 'attending,'

loved of them, not loved of them because it is when applied to dogs, horses, and men, implies dear to them. But the pious or holy is loved by that in some way they are made better. But how the gods because it is pious or holy, which is do pious or holy acts make the gods any better?

equivalent to saying, that it is loved by them Euthyphro explains that he means by pious acts, 5

Euthyphro

acts of service or ministration. Yes; but the min-of piety, or he would never have prosecuted his istrations of the husbandman, the physician, and old father. He is still hoping that he will conde-the builder have an end. To what end do we serve scend to instruct him. But Euthyphro is in a hurry the gods, and what do we help them to accom-and cannot stay. And Socrates' last hope of know-plish? Euthyphro replies, that all these difficult ing the nature of piety before he is prosecuted questions cannot be resolved in a short time; and for impiety has disappeared. As in the he would rather say simply that piety is know-Euthydemus the irony is carried on to the end.

ing how to please the gods in word and deed, by The Euthyphro is manifestly designed to con-prayers and sacrifices. In other words, says trast the real nature of piety and impiety with Socrates, piety is 'a science of asking and giv-the popular conceptions of them. But when the ing'—asking what we want and giving what they popular conceptions of them have been over-want; in short, a mode of doing business between thrown, Socrates does not offer any definition of gods and men. But although they are the givers his own: as in the Laches and Lysis, he prepares of all good, how can we give them any good in the way for an answer to the question which he return? 'Nay, but we give them honour.' Then has raised; but true to his own character, refuses we give them not what is beneficial, but what is to answer himself.

pleasing or dear to them; and this is the point Euthyphro is a religionist, and is elsewhere spo-which has been already disproved.

ken of, if he be the same person, as the author of Socrates, although weary of the subterfuges a philosophy of names, by whose 'prancing and evasions of Euthyphro, remains unshaken steeds' Socrates in the Cratylus is carried away.

in his conviction that he must know the nature He has the conceit and self-confidence of a Soph-6

Euthyphro

ist; no doubt that he is right in prosecuting his his father, who has accidentally been guilty of father has ever entered into his mind. Like a homicide, and is not wholly free from blame. To Sophist too, he is incapable either of framing a purge away the crime appears to him in the light general definition or of following the course of of a duty, whoever may be the criminal.

an argument. His wrong-headedness, one-Thus begins the contrast between the religion sidedness, narrowness, positiveness, are charac-of the letter, or of the narrow and unenlightened teristic of his priestly office. His failure to appre-conscience, and the higher notion of religion hend an argument may be compared to a simi-which Socrates vainly endeavours to elicit from lar defect which is observable in the rhapsode him. 'Piety is doing as I do' is the idea of reli-Ion. But he is not a bad man, and he is friendly gion which first occurs to him, and to many oth-to Socrates, whose familiar sign he recognizes ers who do not say what they think with equal with interest. Though unable to follow him he is frankness. For men are not easily persuaded that very willing to be led by him, and eagerly catches any other religion is better than their own; or at any suggestion which saves him from the that other nations, e.g. the Greeks in the time of trouble of thinking. Moreover he is the enemy of Socrates, were equally serious in their religious Meletus, who, as he says, is availing himself of beliefs and difficulties. The chief difference be-the popular dislike to innovations in religion in tween us and them is, that they were slowly order to injure Socrates; at the same time he is learning what we are in process of forgetting.

amusingly confident that he has weapons in his Greek mythology hardly admitted of the distinc-own armoury which would be more than a match tion between accidental homicide and murder: for him. He is quite sincere in his prosecution of that the pollution of blood was the same in both 7

Euthyphro

cases is also the feeling of the Athenian diviner.

gion arises out of the difficulty of verifying them.

He had not as yet learned the lesson, which phi-There is no measure or standard to which they losophy was teaching, that Homer and Hesiod, can be referred.

if not banished from the state, or whipped out The next definition,
'Piety is that which is of the assembly, as Heracleitus more rudely
pro-loved of the gods,' is shipwrecked on a refined posed, at any rate
were not to be appealed to as distinction between the state and the
act, corre-authorities in religion; and he is ready to defend sponding
respectively to the adjective (philon) his conduct by the examples of
the gods. These and the participle (philoumenon), or rather per-are
the very tales which Socrates cannot abide; haps to the participle and
the verb (philoumenon and his dislike of them, as he suspects, has
and phileitai). The act is prior to the state (as in branded him with the
reputation of impiety. Here Aristotle the energeia precedes the
dunamis); is one answer to the question, 'Why Socrates and the state
of being loved is preceded by the was put to death,' suggested by the
way. An-act of being loved. But piety or holiness is pre-other is
conveyed in the words, 'The Athenians ceded by the act of being
pious, not by the act of do not care about any man being thought wise
being loved; and therefore piety and the state of until he begins to
make other men wise; and then being loved are different. Through
such subtle-for some reason or other they are angry:' which ties of
dialectic Socrates is working his way into may be said to be the rule
of popular toleration a deeper region of thought and feeling. He
means in most other countries, and not at Athens only.

to say that the words 'loved of the gods' ex-In the course of the
argument Socrates remarks press an attribute only, and not the
essence of that the controversial nature of morals and reli-piety.

8

Euthyphro

Then follows the third and last definition, 'Pi-There seem to be altogether three aims or in-ety is a part of justice.' Thus far Socrates has terests in this little Dialogue: (1) the dialectical proceeded in placing religion on a moral founda-development of the idea of piety; (2) the antith-tion. He is seeking to realize the harmony of reli-esis of true and false religion, which is carried to gion and morality, which the great poets a certain extent only; (3) the defence of Socrates.

Aeschylus, Sophocles, and Pindar had uncon-The subtle connection with the Apology and the sciously anticipated, and which is the universal Crito; the holding back of the conclusion, as in want of all men. To this the soothsayer adds the the Charmides, Lysis, Laches, Protagoras, and ceremonial element, 'attending upon the gods.'

other Dialogues; the deep insight into the reli-When further interrogated by Socrates as to the gious world; the dramatic power and play of the nature of this 'attention to the gods,' he replies, two characters; the inimitable irony, are reasons that piety is an affair of business, a science of for believing that the Euthyphro is a genuine Pla-giving and asking, and the like. Socrates points tonic writing. The spirit in which the popular rep-out the anthropomorphism of these notions, (com-resentations of mythology are denounced recalls pare Symp.; Republic; Politicus.) But when we Republic II. The virtue of piety has been already expect him to go on and show that the true ser-mentioned as one of five in the Protagoras, but is vice of the gods is the service of the spirit and the not reckoned among the four cardinal virtues of co-operation with them in all things true and good, Republic IV. The figure of Daedalus has occurred he stops short; this was a lesson which the sooth-in the Meno; that of Proteus in the Euthydemus sayer could not have been made to understand, and Io. The kingly science has already appeared and which every one must learn for himself.

in the Euthydemus, and will reappear in the 9

Euthyphro

Republic and Statesman. But neither from these EUTHYPHRO

nor any other indications of similarity or difference, and still less from arguments respecting by

the suitableness of this little work to aid Socrates at the time of his trial or the reverse, can any Plato

evidence of the date be obtained.

Translated by Benjamin Jowett PERSONS OF THE DIALOGUE: Socrates, Euthyphro.

SCENE: The Porch of the King Archon.

EUTHYPHRO: Why have you left the Lyceum, Socrates? and what are you doing in the Porch of the King Archon? Surely you cannot be concerned in a suit before the King, like myself?

SOCRATES: Not in a suit, Euthyphro; impeach-ment is the word which the Athenians use.

EUTHYPHRO: What! I suppose that some one has been prosecuting you, for I cannot believe that you are the prosecutor of another.

SOCRATES: Certainly not.

10

Euthyphro

EUTHYPHRO: Then some one else has been pros-corrupting his young friends. And of this our ecuting you?

mother the state is to be the judge. Of all our SOCRATES: Yes.

political men he is the only one who seems to EUTHYPHRO: And who is he?

me to begin in the right way, with the cultiva-SOCRATES: A young man who is little known, tion of virtue in youth; like a good husbandman, Euthyphro; and I hardly know him: his name is he makes the young shoots his first care, and Meletus, and he is of the deme of Pitthis. Per-clears away us who are the destroyers of them.

haps you may remember his appearance; he has This is only the first step; he will afterwards at-a beak, and long straight hair, and a beard which tend to the elder branches; and if he goes on as is ill grown.

he has begun, he will be a very great public bene-EUTHYPHRO: No, I do not remember him, factor.

Socrates. But what is the charge which he brings EUTHYPHRO: I hope that he may; but I rather against you?

fear, Socrates, that the opposite will turn out to SOCRATES: What is the charge? Well, a very se-be the truth. My opinion is that in attacking you rious charge, which shows a good deal of char-he is simply aiming a blow at the foundation of acter in the young man, and for which he is cer-the state. But in what way does he say that you tainly not to be despised. He says he knows how corrupt the young?

the youth are corrupted and who are their cor-SOCRATES: He brings a wonderful accusation ruptors. I fancy that he must be a wise man, and against me, which at first hearing excites sur-seeing that I am the reverse of a wise man, he prise: he says that I am a poet or maker of gods, has found me out, and is going to accuse me of and that I invent new gods and deny the exist-11

Euthyphro

ence of old ones; this is the ground of his indict-EUTHYPHRO: I am never likely to try their tem-ment.

per in this way.

EUTHYPHRO: I understand, Socrates; he means SOCRATES: I dare say not, for you are reserved to attack you about the familiar sign which oc-in your behaviour, and seldom impart your wis-casionally, as you say, comes to you. He thinks dom. But I have a benevolent habit of pouring that you are a neologian, and he is going to have out myself to everybody, and would even pay for you up before the court for this. He knows that a listener, and I am afraid that the Athenians such a charge is readily received by the world, may think me too talkative. Now if, as I was say-as I myself know too well; for when I speak in ing, they would only laugh at me, as you say the assembly about divine things, and foretell that they laugh at you, the time might pass gaily the future to them, they laugh at me and think enough in the court; but perhaps they may be in me a madman. Yet every word that I say is true.

earnest, and then what the end will be you sooth-But they are jealous of us all; and we must be sayers only can predict.

brave and go at them.

EUTHYPHRO: I dare say that the affair will end SOCRATES: Their laughter, friend Euthyphro, is in nothing, Socrates, and that you will win your not a matter of much consequence. For a man cause; and I think that I shall win my own.

may be thought wise; but the Athenians, I sus-SOCRATES: And what is your suit, Euthyphro?

pect, do not much trouble themselves about him are you the pursuer or the defendant?

until he begins to impart his wisdom to others, EUTHYPHRO: I am the pursuer.

and then for some reason or other, perhaps, as SOCRATES: Of whom?

you say, from jealousy, they are angry.

EUTHYPHRO: You will think me mad when I tell you.

12

Euthyphro

SOCRATES: Why, has the fugitive wings?

making a distinction between one who is a rela-EUTHYPHRO: Nay, he is not very volatile at his tion and one who is not a relation; for surely the time of life.

pollution is the same in either case, if you know-SOCRATES: Who is he?

ingly associate with the murderer when you EUTHYPHRO: My father.

ought to clear yourself and him by proceeding SOCRATES: Your father! my good man?

against him. The real question is whether the EUTHYPHRO: Yes.

murdered man has been justly slain. If justly, then SOCRATES: And of what is he accused?

your duty is to let the matter alone; but if un-EUTHYPHRO: Of murder, Socrates.

justly, then even if the murderer lives under the SOCRATES: By the powers, Euthyphro! how little same roof with you and eats at the same table, does the common herd know of the nature of proceed against him. Now the man who is dead right and truth. A man must be an extraordi-was a poor dependant of mine who worked for nary man, and have made great strides in wis-us as a field labourer on our farm in Naxos, and dom, before he could have seen his way to bring one day in a fit of drunken passion he got into a such an action.

quarrel with one of our domestic servants and EUTHYPHRO: Indeed, Socrates, he must.

slew him. My father bound him hand and foot SOCRATES: I suppose that the man whom your and threw him into a ditch, and then sent to father murdered was one of your relatives—

Athens to ask of a diviner what he should do clearly he was; for if he had been a stranger you with him. Meanwhile he never attended to him would never have thought of prosecuting him.

and took no care about him, for he regarded him EUTHYPHRO: I am amused, Socrates, at your as a murderer; and thought that no great harm 13

Euthyphro

would be done even if he did die. Now this was men, is his exact knowledge of all such matters.

just what happened. For such was the effect of What should I be good for without it?

cold and hunger and chains upon him, that be-SOCRATES: Rare friend! I think that I cannot do fore the messenger returned from the diviner, better than be your disciple. Then before the trial he was dead. And my father and family are an-with Meletus comes on I shall challenge him, and gry with me for taking the part of the murderer say that I have always had a great interest in re-and prosecuting my father. They say that he did ligious questions, and now, as he charges me with not kill him, and that if he did, the dead man rash imaginations and innovations in religion, I was but a murderer, and I ou ght not to take any have become your disciple. You, Meletus, as I shall notice, for that a son is impious who prosecutes say to him, acknowledge Euthyphro to be a great a father. Which shows, Socrates, how little they theologian, and sound in his opinions; and if you know what the gods think about piety and impi-approve of him you ought to approve of me, and ety.

not have me into court; but if you disapprove, you SOCRATES: Good heavens, Euthyphro! and is should begin by indicting him who is my teacher, your knowledge of religion and of things pious and who will be the ruin, not of the young, but of and impious so very exact, that, supposing the the old; that is to say, of myself whom he instructs, circumstances to be as you state them, you are and of his old father whom he admonishes and not afraid lest you too may be doing an impious chastises. And if Meletus refuses to listen to me, thing in bringing an action against your father?

but will go on, and will not shift the indictment EUTHYPHRO: The best of Euthyphro, and that from me to you, I cannot do better than repeat which distinguishes him, Socrates, from other this challenge in the court.

14

Euthyphro

EUTHYPHRO: Yes, indeed, Socrates; and if he EUTHYPHRO: Piety is doing as I am doing; that attempts to indict me I am mistaken if I do not is to say, prosecuting any one who is guilty of find a flaw in him; the court shall have a great murder, sacrilege, or of any similar crime—

deal more to say to him than to me.

whether he be your father or mother, or who-SOCRATES: And I, my dear friend, knowing this, ever he may be—that makes no difference; and am desirous of becoming your disciple. For I ob-not to prosecute them is impiety. And please to serve that no one appears to notice you—not even consider, Socrates, what a notable proof I will this Meletus; but his sharp eyes have found me give you of the truth of my words, a proof which out at once, and he has indicted me for impiety.

I have already given to others:—of the principle, And therefore, I adjure you to tell me the nature I mean, that the impious, whoever he may be, of piety and impiety, which you said that you ought not to go unpunished. For do not men re-knew so well, and of murder, and of other of-gard Zeus as the best and most righteous of the fences against the gods. What are they? Is not gods?—and yet they admit that he bound his fa-piety in every action always the same? and im-ther (Cronos) because he wickedly devoured his piety, again —is it not always the opposite of pi-sons, and that he too had punished his own fa-ety, and also the same with itself, having, as ther (Uranus) for a similar reason, in a name-impiety, one notion which includes whatever is less manner. And yet when I proceed against my impious?

father, they are angry with me. So inconsistent EUTHYPHRO: To be sure, Socrates.

are they in their way of talking when the gods SOCRATES: And what is piety, and what is impi-are concerned, and when I am concerned.

ety?

SOCRATES: May not this be the reason, 15

Euthyphro

Euthyphro, why I am charged with impiety—that EUTHYPHRO: Yes, Socrates; and, as I was sayI cannot away with these stories about the gods?

ing, I can tell you, if you would like to hear them, and therefore I suppose that people think me many other things about the gods which would wrong. But, as you who are well informed about quite amaze you.

them approve of them, I cannot do better than SOCRATES: I dare say; and you shall tell me them assent to your superior wisdom. What else can I at some other time when I have leisure. But just say, confessing as I do, that I know nothing about at present I would rather hear from you a more them? Tell me, for the love of Zeus, whether you precise answer, which you have not as yet given, really believe that they are true.

my friend, to the question, What is 'piety'?

EUTHYPHRO: Yes, Socrates; and things more When asked, you only replied, Doing as you do, wonderful still, of which the world is in igno-charging your father with murder.

rance.

EUTHYPHRO: And what I said was true, Socrates.

SOCRATES: And do you really believe that the SOCRATES: No doubt, Euthyphro; but you would gods fought with one another, and had dire quar-admit that there are many other pious acts?

rels, battles, and the like, as the poets say, and EUTHYPHRO: There are.

as you may see represented in the works of great SOCRATES: Remember that I did not ask you to give artists? The temples are full of them; and nota-me two or three examples of piety, but to explain the bly the robe of Athene, which is carried up to general idea which makes all pious things to be pious.

the Acropolis at the great Panathenaea, is em-Do you not recollect that there was one idea which broidered with them. Are all these tales of the made the impious impious, and the pious pious?

gods true, Euthyphro?

EUTHYPHRO: I remember.

16

Euthyphro

SOCRATES: Tell me what is the nature of this two being the extreme opposites of one another.

idea, and then I shall have a standard to which I Was not that said?

may look, and by which I may measure actions, EUTHYPHRO: It was.

whether yours or those of any one else, and then SOCRATES: And well said?

I shall be able to say that such and such an ac-EUTHYPHRO: Yes, Socrates, I thought so; it was tion is pious, such another impious.

certainly said.

EUTHYPHRO: I will tell you, if you like.

SOCRATES: And further, Euthyphro, the gods SOCRATES: I should very much like.

were admitted to have enmities and hatreds and EUTHYPHRO: Piety, then, is that which is dear differences?

to the gods, and impiety is that which is not dear EUTHYPHRO: Yes, that was also said.

to them.

SOCRATES: And what sort of difference creates SOCRATES: Very good, Euthyphro; you have now enmity and anger? Suppose for example that you given me the sort of answer which I wanted. But and I, my good friend, differ about a number; do whether what you say is true or not I cannot as differences of this sort make us enemies and set yet tell, although I make no doubt that you will us at variance with one another? Do we not go prove the truth of your words.

at once to arithmetic, and put an end to them EUTHYPHRO: Of course.

by a sum?

SOCRATES: Come, then, and let us examine what EUTHYPHRO: True.

we are saying. That thing or person which is dear SOCRATES: Or suppose that we differ about to the gods is pious, and that thing or person magnitudes, do we not quickly end the differ-which is hateful to the gods is impious, these ences by measuring?

17

Euthyphro

EUTHYPHRO: Very true.

Euthyphro, when they occur, are of a like nature?

SOCRATES: And we end a controversy about EUTHYPHRO: Certainly they are.

heavy and light by resorting to a weighing ma-SOCRATES: They have differences of opinion, as chine?

you say, about good and evil, just and unjust, EUTHYPHRO: To be sure.

honourable and dishonourable: there would have SOCRATES: But what differences are there which been no quarrels among them, if there had been cannot be thus decided, and which therefore no such differences—would there now?

make us angry and set us at enmity with one EUTHYPHRO: You are quite right.

another? I dare say the answer does not occur to SOCRATES: Does not every man love that which you at the moment, and therefore I will suggest he deems noble and just and good, and hate the that these enmities arise when the matters of opposite of them?

difference are the just and unjust, good and evil, EUTHYPHRO: Very true.

honourable and dishonourable. Are not these the SOCRATES: But, as you say, people regard the points about which men differ, and about which same things, some as just and others as unjust,—

when we are unable satisfactorily to decide our about these they dispute; and so there arise wars differences, you and I and all of us quarrel, when and fightings among them.

we do quarrel? (Compare Alcib.) EUTHYPHRO: Very true.

EUTHYPHRO: Yes, Socrates, the nature of the SOCRATES: Then the same things are hated by differences about which we quarrel is such as the gods and loved by the gods, and are both you describe.

hateful and dear to them?

SOCRATES: And the quarrels of the gods, noble EUTHYPHRO: True.

Euthyphro

SOCRATES: And upon this view the same things, that a murderer or any sort of evil-doer ought to Euthyphro, will be pious and also impious?

be let off?

EUTHYPHRO: So I should suppose.

EUTHYPHRO: I should rather say that these are SOCRATES: Then, my friend, I remark with sur-the questions which they are always arguing, prise that you have not answered the question especially in courts of law: they commit all sorts which I asked. For I certainly did not ask you to of crimes, and there is nothing which they will tell me what action is both pious and impious: not do or say in their own defence.

but now it would seem that what is loved by the SOCRATES: But do they admit their guilt, gods is also hated by them. And therefore, Euthyphro, and yet say that they ought not to Euthyphro, in thus chastising your father you be punished?

may very likely be doing what is agreeable to EUTHYPHRO: No; they do not.

Zeus but disagreeable to Cronos or Uranus, and SOCRATES: Then there are some things which what is acceptable to Hephaestus but unaccept-they do not venture to say and do: for they do able to Here, and there may be other gods who not venture to argue that the guilty are to be have similar differences of opinion.

unpunished, but they deny their guilt, do they EUTHYPHRO: But I believe, Socrates, that all the not?

gods would be agreed as to the propriety of pun-EUTHYPHRO: Yes.

ishing a murderer: there would be no difference SOCRATES: Then they do not argue that the evil-of opinion about that.

doer should not be punished, but they argue SOCRATES: Well, but speaking of men, about the fact of who the evil-doer is, and what Euthyphro, did you ever hear any one arguing he did and when?

19

Euthyphro

EUTHYPHRO: True.

ers of the gods what he ought to do with him, SOCRATES: And the gods are in the same case, dies unjustly; and that on behalf of such an one if as you assert they quarrel about just and un-a son ought to proceed against his father and just, and some of them say while others deny accuse him of murder. How would you show that that injustice is done among them. For surely all the gods absolutely agree in approving of his neither God nor man will ever venture to say act? Prove to me that they do, and I will applaud that the doer of injustice is not to be punished?

your wisdom as long as I live.

EUTHYPHRO: That is true, Socrates, in the main.

EUTHYPHRO: It will be a difficult task; but I could SOCRATES: But they join issue about the particu-make the matter very clear indeed to you.

lars—gods and men alike; and, if they dispute at SOCRATES: I understand; you mean to say that I all, they dispute about some act which is called am not so quick of apprehension as the judges: in question, and which by some is affirmed to be for to them you will be sure to prove that the act just, by others to be unjust. Is not that true?

is unjust, and hateful to the gods.

EUTHYPHRO: Quite true.

EUTHYPHRO: Yes indeed, Socrates; at least if SOCRATES: Well then, my dear friend Euthyphro, they will listen to me.

do tell me, for my better instruction and infor-SOCRATES: But they will be sure to listen if they mation, what proof have you that in the opinion find that you are a good speaker. There was a of all the gods a servant who is guilty of murder, notion that came into my mind while you were and is put in chains by the master of the dead speaking; I said to myself: 'Well, and what if man, and dies because he is put in chains before Euthyphro does prove to me that all the gods he who bound him can learn from the interpret-regarded the death of the serf as unjust, how do 20

Euthyphro

I know anything more of the nature of piety and gods love is pious and holy, and the opposite impiety? for granting that this action may be which they all hate, impious.

hateful to the gods, still piety and impiety are SOCRATES: Ought we to enquire into the truth not adequately defined by these distinctions, for of this, Euthyphro, or simply to accept the mere that which is hateful to the gods has been shown statement on our own authority and that of oth-to be also pleasing and dear to them.' And there-ers? What do you say?

fore, Euthyphro, I do not ask you to prove this; I EUTHYPHRO: We should enquire; and I believe will suppose, if you like, that all the gods con-that the statement will stand the test of enquiry.

demn and abominate such an action. But I will SOCRATES: We shall know better, my good friend, amend the definition so far as to say that what in a little while. The point which I should first all the gods hate is impious, and what they love wish to understand is whether the pious or holy pious or holy; and what some of them love and is beloved by the gods because it is holy, or holy others hate is both or neither. Shall this be our because it is beloved of the gods.

definition of piety and impiety?

EUTHYPHRO: I do not understand your mean-EUTHYPHRO: Why not, Socrates?

ing, Socrates.

SOCRATES: Why not! certainly, as far as I am SOCRATES: I will endeavour to explain: we, speak concerned, Euthyphro, there is no reason why of carrying and we speak of being carried, of lead-not. But whether this admission will greatly asing and being led, seeing and being seen. You sist you in the task of instructing me as you prom-know that in all such cases there is a difference, ised, is a matter for you to consider.

and you know also in what the difference lies?

EUTHYPHRO: Yes, I should say that what all the EUTHYPHRO: I think that I understand.

21

Euthyphro

SOCRATES: And is not that which is beloved dis-state of suffering,
but it is in a state of suffering tinct from that which loves?

because it suffers. Do you not agree?

EUTHYPHRO: Certainly.

EUTHYPHRO: Yes.

SOCRATES: Well; and now tell me, is that which SOCRATES: Is not
that which is loved in some is carried in this state of carrying
because it is state either of becoming or suffering?

carried, or for some other reason?

EUTHYPHRO: Yes.

EUTHYPHRO: No; that is the reason.

SOCRATES: And the same holds as in the previ-SOCRATES: And the
same is true of what is led ous instances; the state of being loved
follows and of what is seen?

the act of being loved, and not the act the state.

EUTHYPHRO: True.

EUTHYPHRO: Certainly.

SOCRATES: And a thing is not seen because it is SOCRATES: And what do you say of piety, visible, but conversely, visible because it is seen; Euthyphro: is not piety, according to your defini-nor is a thing led because it is in the state of tion, loved by all the gods?

being led, or carried because it is in the state of EUTHYPHRO: Yes.

being carried, but the converse of this. And now SOCRATES: Because it is pious or holy, or for some I think, Euthyphro, that my meaning will be in-other reason?

telligible; and my meaning is, that any state of EUTHYPHRO: No, that is the reason.

action or passion implies previous action or pas-SOCRATES: It is loved because it is holy, not holy sion. It does not become because it is becoming, because it is loved?

but it is in a state of becoming because it be-EUTHYPHRO: Yes.

comes; neither does it suffer because it is in a SOCRATES: And that which is dear to the gods 22

Euthyphro

is loved by them, and is in a state to be loved of God is dear to him
because loved by him, then them because it is loved of them?

that which is holy would have been holy because EUTHYPHRO:
Certainly.

loved by him. But now you see that the reverse SOCRATES: Then
that which is dear to the gods, is the case, and that they are quite
different from Euthyphro, is not holy, nor is that which is holy one
another. For one (theophiles) is of a kind to loved of God, as you
affirm; but they are two be loved cause it is loved, and the other
(osion) different things.

is loved because it is of a kind to be loved. Thus EUTHYPHRO: How
do you mean, Socrates?

you appear to me, Euthyphro, when I ask you SOCRATES: I mean to
say that the holy has been what is the essence of holiness, to offer an
at-acknowledged by us to be loved of God because tribute only, and
not the essence—the attribute it is holy, not to be holy because it is
loved.

of being loved by all the gods. But you still refuse EUTHYPHRO:
Yes.

to explain to me the nature of holiness. And SOCRATES: But that
which is dear to the gods is therefore, if you please, I will ask you
not to hide dear to them because it is loved by them, not your
treasure, but to tell me once more what loved by them because it is
dear to them.

holiness or piety really is, whether dear to the EUTHYPHRO: True.

gods or not (for that is a matter about which we SOCRATES: But,
friend Euthyphro, if that which will not quarrel); and what is
impiety?

is holy is the same with that which is dear to EUTHYPHRO: I really
do not know, Socrates, how God, and is loved because it is holy, then
that to express what I mean. For somehow or other which is dear to
God would have been loved as our arguments, on whatever ground
we rest them, being dear to God; but if that which is dear to seem to
turn round and walk away from us.

23

Euthyphro

SOCRATES: Your words, Euthyphro, are like the of this. As I perceive that you are lazy, I will handiwork of my ancestor Daedalus; and if I were myself endeavour to show you how you might the sayer or propounder of them, you might say instruct me in the nature of piety; and I hope that my arguments walk away and will not re-that you will not grudge your labour. Tell me, main fixed where they are placed because I am then—Is not that which is pious necessarily just?

a descendant of his. But now, since these notions EUTHYPHRO: Yes.

are your own, you must find some other gibe, SOCRATES: And is, then, all which is just pious?

for they certainly, as you yourself allow, show an or, is that which is pious all just, but that which inclination to be on the move.

is just, only in part and not all, pious?

EUTHYPHRO: Nay, Socrates, I shall still say that EUTHYPHRO: I do not understand you, Socrates.

you are the Daedalus who sets arguments in SOCRATES: And yet I know that you are as much motion; not I, certainly, but you make them move wiser than I am, as you are younger. But, as I or go round, for they would never have stirred, was saying, revered friend, the abundance of as far as I am concerned.

your wisdom makes you lazy. Please to exert your-SOCRATES: Then I must be a greater than self, for there is no real difficulty in understand-Daedalus: for whereas he only made his own in-ing me. What I mean I may explain by an illus-ventions to move, I move those of other people tration of what I do not mean. The poet as well. And the beauty of it is, that I would (Stasinus) sings—

rather not. For I would give the wisdom of

'Of Zeus, the author and creator of all Daedalus, and the wealth of Tantalus, to be able these things, You will not tell: for where to detain them and keep them fixed. But enough there is fear there is also reverence.'

24

Euthyphro

Now I disagree with this poet. Shall I tell you in notion than the odd. I suppose that you follow what respect?

me now?

EUTHYPHRO: By all means.

EUTHYPHRO: Quite well.

SOCRATES: I should not say that where there is SOCRATES: That was the sort of question which fear there is also reverence; for I am sure that I meant to raise when I asked whether the just many persons fear poverty and disease, and the is always the pious, or the pious always the just; like evils, but I do not perceive that they rever- and whether there may not be justice where ence the objects of their fear.

there is not piety; for justice is the more extended EUTHYPHRO: Very true.

notion of which piety is only a part. Do you dis-SOCRATES: But where reverence is, there is fear; sent?

for he who has a feeling of reverence and shame EUTHYPHRO: No, I think that you are quite right.

about the commission of any action, fears and is SOCRATES: Then, if piety is a part of justice, I afraid of an ill reputation.

suppose that we should enquire what part? If EUTHYPHRO: No doubt.

you had pursued the enquiry in the previous SOCRATES: Then we are wrong in saying that cases; for instance, if you had asked me what is where there is fear there is also reverence; and an even number, and what part of number the we should say, where there is reverence there is even is, I should have had no difficulty in reply- also fear. But there is not always reverence where ing, a number which represents a figure having there is fear; for fear is a more extended notion, two equal sides. Do you not agree?

and reverence is a part of fear, just as the odd is EUTHYPHRO: Yes, I quite agree.

a part of number, and number is a more extended SOCRATES: In like manner, I want you to tell me 25

Euthyphro

what part of justice is piety or holiness, that I EUTHYPHRO: Yes.

may be able to tell Meletus not to do me injus-SOCRATES: Nor is every one qualified to attend tice, or indict me for impiety, as I am now ad-to dogs, but only the huntsman?

equately instructed by you in the nature of pi-EUTHYPHRO: True.

ety or holiness, and their opposites.

SOCRATES: And I should also conceive that the EUTHYPHRO: Piety or holiness, Socrates, appears art of the huntsman is the art of attending to to me to be that part of justice which attends to dogs?

the gods, as there is the other part of justice EUTHYPHRO: Yes.

which attends to men.

SOCRATES: As the art of the oxherd is the art of SOCRATES: That is good, Euthyphro; yet still attending to oxen?

there is a little point about which I should like to EUTHYPHRO: Very true.

have further information, What is the meaning SOCRATES: In like manner holiness or piety is of 'attention'? For attention can hardly be used the art of attending to the gods?—that would be in the same sense when applied to the gods as your meaning, Euthyphro?

when applied to other things. For instance, EUTHYPHRO: Yes.

horses are said to require attention, and not ev-SOCRATES: And is not attention always designed ery person is able to attend to them, but only a for the good or benefit of that to which the at-person skilled in horsemanship. Is it not so?

tention is given? As in the case of horses, you EUTHYPHRO:
Certainly.

may observe that when attended to by the SOCRATES: I should
suppose that the art of horse-horseman's art they are benefited and
im-manship is the art of attending to horses?

proved, are they not?

Euthyphro

EUTHYPHRO: True.

SOCRATES: Good: but I must still ask what is SOCRATES: As the dogs are benefited by the this attention to the gods which is called piety?

huntsman's art, and the oxen by the art of the EUTHYPHRO: It is such, Socrates, as servants oxherd, and all other things are tended or at-show to their masters.

tended for their good and not for their hurt?

SOCRATES: I understand—a sort of ministration EUTHYPHRO: Certainly, not for their hurt.

to the gods.

SOCRATES: But for their good?

EUTHYPHRO: Exactly.

EUTHYPHRO: Of course.

SOCRATES: Medicine is also a sort of ministra-SOCRATES: And does piety or holiness, which tion or service, having in view the attainment of has been defined to be the art of attending to some object—would you not say of health?

the gods, benefit or improve them? Would you EUTHYPHRO: I should.

say that when you do a holy act you make any of SOCRATES: Again, there is an art which minis-the gods better?

ters to the ship-builder with a view to the attain-EUTHYPHRO: No, no; that was certainly not what ment of some result?

I meant.

EUTHYPHRO: Yes, Socrates, with a view to the SOCRATES: And I, Euthyphro, never supposed building of a ship.

that you did. I asked you the question about the SOCRATES: As there is an art which ministers to nature of the attention, because I thought that the house-builder with a view to the building of you did not.

a house?

EUTHYPHRO: You do me justice, Socrates; that EUTHYPHRO: Yes.

is not the sort of attention which I mean.

SOCRATES: And now tell me, my good friend, 27

about the art which ministers to the gods: what EUTHYPHRO: I have told you already, Socrates, work does that help to accomplish? For you must that to learn all these things accurately will be surely know if, as you say, you are of all men very tiresome. Let me simply say that piety or living the one who is best instructed in religion.

holiness is learning how to please the gods in EUTHYPHRO: And I speak the truth, Socrates.

word and deed, by prayers and sacrifices. Such SOCRATES: Tell me then, oh tell me—what is that piety is the salvation of families and states, just fair work which the gods do by the help of our as the impious, which is unpleasing to the gods, ministrations?

is their ruin and destruction.

EUTHYPHRO: Many and fair, Socrates, are the SOCRATES: I think that you could have answered works which they do.

in much fewer words the chief question which I SOCRATES: Why, my friend, and so are those of asked, Euthyphro, if you had chosen. But I see a general. But the chief of them is easily told.

plainly that you are not disposed to instruct me—

Would you not say that victory in war is the chief clearly not: else why, when we reached the point, of them?

did you turn aside? Had you only answered me I EUTHYPHRO: Certainly.

should have truly learned of you by this time SOCRATES: Many and fair, too, are the works of the nature of piety. Now, as the asker of a ques-the husbandman, if I am not mistaken; but his chief tion is necessarily dependent on the answerer, work is the production of food from the earth?

whither he leads I must follow; and can only ask EUTHYPHRO: Exactly.

again, what is the pious, and what is piety? Do SOCRATES: And of the many and fair things done you mean that they are a sort of science of pray-by the gods, which is the chief or principal one?

ing and sacrificing?

28

Euthyphro

EUTHYPHRO: Yes, I do.

would be no meaning in an art which gives to SOCRATES: And sacrificing is giving to the gods, any one that which he does not want.

and prayer is asking of the gods?

EUTHYPHRO: Very true, Socrates.

EUTHYPHRO: Yes, Socrates.

SOCRATES: Then piety, Euthyphro, is an art SOCRATES: Upon this view, then, piety is a sci-which gods and men have of doing business with ence of asking and giving?

one another?

EUTHYPHRO: You understand me capitally, EUTHYPHRO: That is an expression which you Socrates.

may use, if you like.

SOCRATES: Yes, my friend; the reason is that I SOCRATES: But I have no particular liking for am a votary of your science, and give my mind anything but the truth. I wish, however, that you to it, and therefore nothing which you say will would tell me what benefit accrues to the gods be thrown away upon me. Please then to tell me, from our gifts. There is no doubt about what they what is the nature of this service to the gods?

give to us; for there is no good thing which they Do you mean that we prefer requests and give do not give; but how we can give any good thing gifts to them?

to them in return is far from being equally clear.

EUTHYPHRO: Yes, I do.

If they give everything and we give nothing, that SOCRATES: Is not the right way of asking to ask must be an affair of business in which we have of them what we want?

very greatly the advantage of them.

EUTHYPHRO: Certainly.

EUTHYPHRO: And do you imagine, Socrates, that SOCRATES: And the right way of giving is to give any benefit accrues to the gods from our gifts?

to them in return what they want of us. There SOCRATES: But if not, Euthyphro, what is the 29 meaning of gifts which are conferred by us upon not the same with that which is loved of the the gods?

gods? Have you forgotten?

EUTHYPHRO: What else, but tributes of honour; EUTHYPHRO: I quite remember.

and, as I was just now saying, what pleases SOCRATES: And are you not saying that what is them?

loved of the gods is holy; and is not this the same SOCRATES: Piety, then, is pleasing to the gods, as what is dear to them—do you see?

but not beneficial or dear to them?

EUTHYPHRO: True.

EUTHYPHRO: I should say that nothing could be SOCRATES: Then either we were wrong in our dearer.

former assertion; or, if we were right then, we SOCRATES: Then once more the assertion is re-are wrong now.

peated that piety is dear to the gods?

EUTHYPHRO: One of the two must be true.

EUTHYPHRO: Certainly.

SOCRATES: Then we must begin again and ask, SOCRATES: And when you say this, can you won-What is piety? That is an enquiry which I shall der at your words not standing firm, but walk-never be weary of pursuing as far as in me lies; ing away? Will you accuse me of being the and I entreat you not to scorn me, but to apply Daedalus who makes them walk away, not per-your mind to the utmost, and tell me the truth.

ceiving that there is another and far greater art-For, if any man knows, you are he; and therefore ist than Daedalus who makes them go round in I must detain you, like Proteus, until you tell. If a circle, and he is yourself; for the argument, as you had not certainly known the nature of piety you will perceive, comes round to the same point.

and impiety, I am confident that you would never, Were we not saying that the holy or pious was on behalf of a serf, have charged your aged fa-30

Euthyphro

ther with murder. You would not have run such a risk of doing wrong in the sight of the gods, and you would have had too much respect for the opinions of men. I am sure, therefore, that If you wish to view more of you know the nature of piety and impiety. Speak Plato's works in PDF, be sure out then, my dear Euthyphro, and do not hide to return to your knowledge.